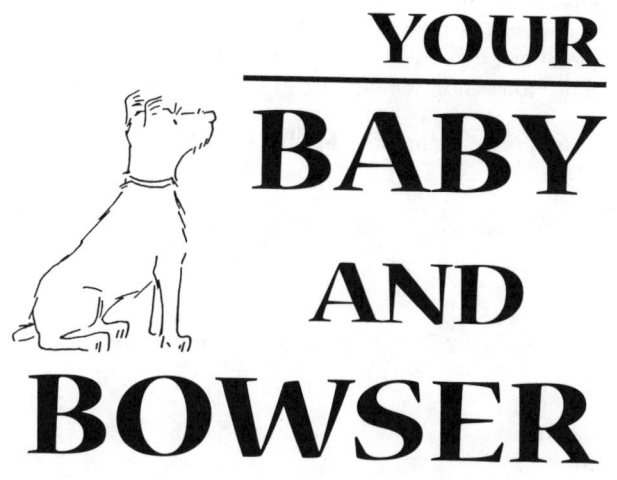

YOUR
BABY
AND
BOWSER

Stephen C. Rafe

Illustrations by Kathy Murphy Dunn

Alpine
Blue Ribbon Books
Loveland, Color

D1378217

Your Baby and Bowser
Copyright © 2004 by Stephen C. Rafe
Original edition copyrighted 1990 as *Your New Baby and Bowser* by William Denlinger.

Library of Congress Cataloging-in-Publication Data

Rafe, Stephen C.
   Your baby and Bowser / Stephen C. Rafe ; illustrations by Kathy Murphy Dunn.
      p. cm.
   ISBN 1-57779-045-6
    1. Dogs--Behavior. 2. Infants. 3. Dogs--Training. 4. Dogs--Social aspects. I. Title.

   SF433.R339 2004
   636.7--dc22
                                      2004052920

The information contained in this book is complete and accurate to the best of our knowledge. All recommendations are made without guarantee on the part of the author or Alpine Publications, Inc. The author and publisher disclaim any liability with the use of this information.

This book is available at special quantity discounts for breeders and for club promotions, premiums, or educational use. Write for details.

For the sake of simplicity, the terms "he" or "she" are sometimes used to identify an animal or person. These are used in the generic sense only. No discrimination of any kind is intended toward either sex.

Many manufacturers secure trademark rights for their products. When Alpine Publications is aware of a trademark claim, we identify the product name by using initial capital letters.

Cover Design: Laura Newport
Cover Photo: © Click the Photo Connection
Editing: Betty J. McKinney
Layout: Laura Newport
Illustrations: Kathy Murphy Dunn

First printing 2004

1 2 3 4 5 6 7 8 9 0

Printed in the United States of America.

Contents

Foreword

Every dog owner should read this book, but if you have—or expect to have—children or grandchildren, then this book's preventative wisdom is as necessary as fire insurance. Mr. Rafe is a leading authority on canine behavior. He also understands the literature in two relevant areas of experimental psychology: animal learning and behavior modification. With this background, the author produces clear and practical advice that can help save children from being disfigured, dogs from being euthanized, and parents/owners from going through traumatic experiences.

Richard K. Lore, Ph.D.
(Retired) Professor of Psychology and
Vice Chair of Graduate Studies
Rutgers University

Preface

If you are a dog owner who is planning a family, is an expectant parent or has just brought home a new baby or adopted child, you probably have concerns about how your dog will respond to the new addition. If your family situation has changed in any other way that involves bringing dogs and children together, you may also have concerns, and for good reason: More than two million children are bitten by dogs each year. Most of these bites take place in the children's own homes.

Should you get rid of your dogs? With proper understanding of canine behavior and adequate preparation, most of these tragic situations can be prevented. If you are a dog owner with concerns about keeping your dog because of children, grandchildren or your friend's children, rest assured—you can teach your dog not only to accept children, but also to behave in a safe and consistent manner around them. Do not, however, expect it to happen automatically. It requires socializing and conditioning your dog, and even examining your own relationship with him

In this book I share observations on the effect that owners' personalities have on a dog's behavior. I will teach you how use a dog's own signals (body language) to establish and maintain leadership. I will explain how proven principles of behavior modification can help you prepare your dog to meet a child, prevent jealousy and inappropriate guarding behavior, and mold your dog into a safe companion. Together, these techniques will help adults raise children and dogs together successfully.

The guidance contained in this book is intended for most dogs and their owners and should be followed in its entirety. Since dog behavior is subject to many variables beyond the scope of this book, the publishing of this book must not be considered an assumption of liability by the author, publisher or artist. However, if you follow the guidance herein, you can expect things to go much more smoothly when "Bowser meets Baby."

Stephen C. Rafe
September 2004

PART I

WHEN BOWSER MEETS BABY

Planning a Successful Introduction

Joy or Disaster?
It's Up to You

Bringing the family dog and a new baby, or a new dog and young children, together for the first time can be traumatic for all concerned, or it can be a joy. Many dog owners are anxious during these circumstances. The concerns are justified! For one thing, the family dog may have defined the home as his territory to be protected from all intruders. For another, most dogs are naturally concerned about anything that squeals or wiggles. At the extreme, if left untrained and unchecked, a dog might regard an infant as an animal to be killed, as a rag doll toy to be played with (which could be fatal), or as a helpless puppy that the dog may try to pick up by the neck (which could kill a baby).

We do not mean to be alarmists, but this concern has been expressed in many books on animal behavior. Dr. Michael W. Fox, writing as Director of the Institute for the Study of Animal Problems of The Humane Society of the United States, in his book, *Understanding Your Dog* (Bantam Books, NY, 1981 ed.), discusses prey chasing behavior as part of the hunting reflex—especially in sporting breeds of dogs. He says, "And so the dog, having chased the 'prey,' has to bite and kill it." He refers to mailmen and children, but the same holds true for infants since dogs do not discriminate unless they are properly taught.

Most owners wait until the baby arrives or a new dog has been acquired and then bring the family and Bowser together in a calm, quiet environment. They allow Bowser to sniff while the parents hold the newcomer and pet Bowser gently. They might repeat the procedure a few times, and that's it.

Always Prepare in Advance

These steps are fine, but most dog owners will want to do more—and they should. The first step to introducing the family dog to a new baby (or newly adopted youngster, for that matter) should begin months before the child's actual arrival. It begins with making sure that your dog is properly trained and socialized. Parents must learn to read their dog's signals and evaluate the ways that their own personality and family dynamics affect the dog's behavior.

For this program to work well, both parents must have a positive rapport with the dog, and the dog should perceive them as leaders. In a family where people are either overly coddling or overly disciplinarian, the dog could become a problem. For example, he might be too dominant, spoiled, or insecure to accept the baby. We'll start with building the proper rapport, then proceed to making the actual introductions, and finally, we will discuss training basic commands and dealing with common problems that can occur when children and dogs share the same household.

There should be no rough play with the dog. It encourages the dog to play roughly with the child. Also, there should be no yelling or hitting among people in the house. Dogs copy human behavior; like children, they learn from what they observe.

A dog that is overly possessive can also be a problem, especially when a child is in the toddler stage and may interfere with the dog's meal or try to take a toy from him.

Keep your dog on leash and teach him to always sit before children are allowed to pet him. Praise him for good behavior. Photo © Judith Strom.

Socializing Bowser

If your dog is not already obedience trained, that is the place to begin. At the very least, he should know such commands as sit, down, heel, come, no or leave it, and enough.

"Leave it" tells him not to touch. "Enough" tells him to stop doing something, such as barking, nudging, and so on. Also, be sure to say "Off," not "Down," when you intend it to mean something like "Get off me" or "Get off the furniture." Use "Down" only to mean "Lie down."

Never use your dog's name in a scolding way. Otherwise he will learn to associate his name with negative experiences and may avoid you when he hears it.

Allow your dog to be around people as much as possible, but do not overindulge him with excessive petting. He needs to learn how to be with people and yet be left alone without nudging, pawing, or vocalizing for attention. Take him to a wide variety of places. Playgrounds, parks, school yards, shopping centers, office parks, and the like provide experiences that will help your dog accept anything new—even a baby. At first, stay far away from people when you visit each location. Gradually, over several visits, start walking him closer to people and other animals.

Keep your dog on a loose leash during each outing, and always take him through his obedience commands while at each new location. Teach him that he must sit to "say hello" to people. Begin with introducing your dog to adults, and eventually teach him to always sit before children are allowed to pet him.

Expect good behavior from Bowser at all times and you will be more likely to get it. Praise his positive responses when they occur and he will be more inclined to repeat them.

7

Practice the following exercise with adults *before* you expose your dog to children. Tell the dog to "Sit." If he does, allow the person to pet him as you say "Good sit." If he doesn't sit, or tries to jump up, say "Off" and tighten the leash to keep the dog from making contact with the person. Heel the dog away. Keep him walking in the other direction for at least ten seconds. Then return and try again. Do this no more than three times in a row, and allow at least fifteen minutes between sessions.

If the dog doesn't seem to be learning to sit to be petted on command within a reasonable number of attempts, consult a qualified obedience trainer or behaviorist for help. It is *essential* that you have this kind of control before you bring home a new baby.

Introducing Toddlers

When you are ready to work with your dog around young children, at first introduce him to them outside the home—away from his own territory. Again, always keep your dog on a leash. Neutral areas such as a park are good locations for doing this. Once you are certain Bowser will behave properly around young children away from your property, allow him to greet youngsters at your property. Once that is successful, do the same inside the house.

A dog that is socialized to a wide variety of people, locations, and experiences will be more likely to accept your new baby successfully.

Understanding
Bowser's Personality

The personalities of dogs can be divided into four basic groups based upon classic approach/avoidance signals. The concept for defining four basic personalities is not new; it dates back to Hippocrates, who applied it to people some 2,400 years ago. He referred to them as Sanguine, Choleric, Phlegmatic, and Melancholy. The traits that he used to describe each human personality fit quite well into my personality model for dogs, even though the intensity of the signals may change with specific events. I call these four distinct categories:

Approach I – I want to approach you (Active)
Approach II – I would accept your approach (Passive)
Avoidance I – I want to keep you away from me (Active)
Avoidance II – I want to keep me away from you (Passive)

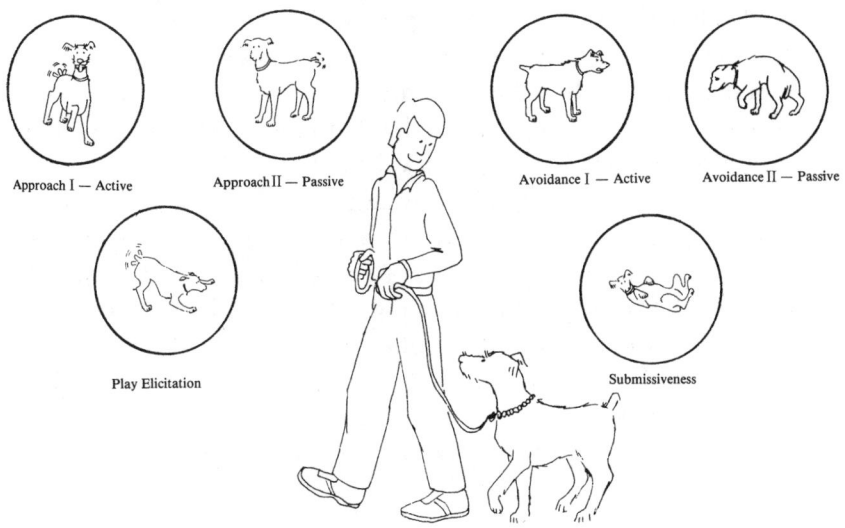

Approach I — Active   Approach II — Passive   Avoidance I — Active   Avoidance II — Passive

Play Elicitation   Submissiveness

This Sheltie is allowing the child's gentle approach. Photo © Robert and Eunice Pearcy.

Interpreting Your Dog's Signals

When dogs want to communicate a desire to approach or avoid other members of their species, they use body language and vocalizations that other dogs clearly understand. Dogs use the same signals when they communicate with people; however, people frequently miss or misunderstand these signals. Often the result is a confrontation that could have been avoided.

When you understand your dog's basic signals, learn to read their intensity, and come to know how your dog reads your nonverbal messages, you are on your way to establishing a better relationship with your pet. This knowledge will help you remove the uncertainty about how you should respond to your dog and help you deal with new or unfamiliar situations more effectively.

How do we recognize these signals? How do we know what a dog's body language is telling us?

Approach

In general, an Approach I dog will demonstrate exuberance and may advance toward you with a "friendly" face and tail. His gait will be jaunty, or even bounding. The head will be high, the tail will wag in a high position, and so on. When closer to you, the dog may retract his lips horizontally into a "smile," his tongue may protrude slightly, and the dog may make nudging motions in the air with his head. If restrained by a leash, crate, or kennel, he may prance up and down and bark excitedly.

Upon contact, the Approach I dog may become less animated, crouch slightly, and hold his tail a little lower while continuing to wag it. If the dog feels confident with your contact, he may resume the earlier signals or postures. An overly submissive dog may roll over or even release a small amount of urine.

An Approach II dog may demonstrate restrained enthusiasm and maintain a relatively greater physical distance while still showing a friendly, although more submissive, face and tail. For example, he may turn his body in excited circles but not advance toward you. He may be less animated than an Approach I dog if

Approach I   Approach II

you try to approach him. The Approach II dog may make some eye contact, but will quickly look away. He will usually carry his head and tail lower than the Approach I dog, and may wag the tail somewhat less. When he does approach you, if at all, he may turn his body slightly sideways as he walks.

Upon contact, he may avert his gaze even further and raise one paw. He may be more likely than the Approach I dog to roll over and discharge a small amount of urine.

Play Elicitation

Either an Approach I dog or an Approach II dog may elicit play once he is confident around you. The signals for play include lowering the front end into a "bowing" position; raising the front paws; bounding in place; a more pronounced tail-wagging, "chase me" gesture made while still remaining nearby; and, possibly, playful nips in the air. Either type of dog, when content, may hold his lips in a "grin" or relax his mouth entirely. The eyelids may be slightly closed. The overall expression may look as though the dog has just experienced the pleasure associated with scratching an itch. Such a dog will often sit or lie down close by and respond positively to friendly contact.

12

Avoidance

An Avoidance I dog will approach, often with deliberate movements, standing tall, and incorporating other postures that are associated with aggression. These may include: mouth slightly open, teeth displayed, direct stare, stiff legs to display more height, raised hackles, ears up and directed forward, lips drawn to expose the canine teeth, head high with neck arched, tail held high with the tip flagging briskly over a short distance, low growling or snarling, and short, advancing motions. Such a dog may also urinate and scrape the ground briskly.

If you move closer and the dog drops his tail somewhat and shifts his weight to his hind feet, he may not want to carry out an attack unless threatened. If the dog continues to display an aggressive front, but changes the rear to more submissive postures, he may be in conflict over one of the following: aggression vs. fear (fight/flight), submissiveness or friendliness vs. self-protectiveness, or curiosity vs. fear or uncertainty.

If an Avoidance I dog attacks, he will most often align himself toward you, lower his head, extend the neck, drop the ears back and lunge.

By contrast, an Avoidance II dog will withdraw and display postures associated with fear, including those that appear to decrease his size. He will generally tuck his tail tightly between

Avoidance I

Avoidance II

the legs, flatten the ears back against the head, display a *slight* grin, dart the eyes back and forth as though looking for a place to retreat, turn his body slightly away from you, lower the head, and possibly raise the hackles slightly.

Are Signals Reliable?

Studies show that all members of a species tend to understand each other's signals and this is true among dogs, even allowing for extreme differences in breeds. Of course, once you get beyond the overall, general signals, a lot of fine-tuning can take place. The body language of a fearful dog (Avoidance II) that turns aggressive differs from that of a dominant dog that becomes aggressive (Avoidance I).

A dog that guards aggressively, or one that is aggressively overprotective, may also have a dominant personality. However, the guarding or overprotecting signals will be slightly different from those of a dog that displays dominance aggression.

Even within overprotective aggression, for example, the postures may vary depending on what, or whom, the dog is overprotecting and what or who is stimulating the dog's aggressive behavior. The signals of a dog that overprotects his food bowl *from* his owners exhibits different signals from those of dog that overprotects the owners themselves.

This fine-tuning goes beyond stereotyped aggressive signals and enables the animal to communicate the intensity, as well as the nature, of his behavior. While survival of the species dictates that dogs must understand these nuances, people generally don't observe the differences very well, until someone points them out. In fact, even skilled observers may miss entire canine "dialogues" consisting of several small adjustments in posture that occur rapidly in a specific order.

Learning to classify your dog's disposition into the four classic approach/avoidance behaviors and observing the nuances of his body language will help immensely when you are working with him and your child.

Your Personality
Affects Bowser's Behavior

Understanding how your personality
influences your dog's behavior is one of the
most important steps in having Bowser meet
baby successfully. Have you ever thought about
the consequences of your own actions when you are with your
dog? Have you considered how he interprets the messages
you are sending him each time you play with him, give him
treats, and so on? Most owners have no idea of how the dog
sees their actions, and no understanding of how their actions
affect their dogs' behavior. Many dogs that owners call "bossy,"

*Your relationship with
your dog is the predic-
tor of his success with
your baby. Photo ©
Judith Strom.*

or, at the other extreme, "frightened of their own shadow," may actually be victims of an improper relationship between owner and dog. Dogs are relatively simple creatures and most of them do their best to cope with everyday life in the home. Basically, they react to their environment and to the way they are treated.

Your relationship with your dog is a predictor of his success with your baby. You should love your dogs, but sometimes you have to practice a kind of "tough love"—love that is neither disciplinarian nor coddling, but fair and consistent. We all learned better from the teacher who was friendly, or who "understood" us, yet never gave in to us when we were wrong.

Owners who overly display either their own aggression (through play or punishment), or their own need for affection (through coddling and bribing) can cause a dog to "fail" in his relationship with the family. Don't sabotage your relationship with your dog. Learn *how* to deal with him in ways he understands. Do not become the domineering owner, on one end of the scale, nor the overindulgent owner, at the other end.

The Domineering Owner

The domineering owner frequently plays with the dog in a rough manner. Tug-of-war is a common game that often ends with the owner intimidating the dog in order to "win." It also increases the power of a dog's bite. In fact, all aggressive games can make the dog a poor performer in training.

 Rule:

Do nothing that may cause the dog to challenge your leadership. No tug-of-war, no wrestling, no pushing the dog away to cause him to bound back at you. And certainly, no slapping the dog around in "play."

Roughhouse activities actually invite dogs to challenge their owners. First, you must win the game if you want to maintain control. Second, in causing the dog to lose, you may be intimidating the dog and making him equally untrainable.

Physical force or harsh punishment rarely corrects a dog's so-called misbehaviors. Actually, when you think about it, most behaviors are not "bad" in terms of what dogs do naturally. We just don't happen to like when, or where, they do them.

For example, urinating and defecating is a natural act for a dog. It only makes us angry when he does it in places we don't approve of. Is soiling the real problem? No, it is the lack of training that is at fault. The same holds true of dogs that raid garbage cans, steal from counters, chew on furniture, and so on. It is a dog's nature to forage, locate food, and chew. Again, when it displeases us, it is because we just don't happen to like when and where the behavior is taking place.

Sticking a dog's nose in his feces to correct house soiling does not work. Bashing the dog with rolled-up newspapers for almost any misbehavior is also destined to fail. In fact, with many dogs, that can trigger a sight-bite reflex toward any fast-moving object.

Some discipline-oriented owners punish their dogs by locking them in basements or laundry rooms, or by depriving them of dinner that night. Incredible as it may seem, one owner previously tried beating the dog *before* leaving the house each day, as a "warning" to the dog to behave. Domineering owners also frequently scream at their dogs, using the dog's name in the process. The yelling intimidates the dog; it does not make him obey. Using his name while yelling teaches him to associate his name with punishment.

Quite often, dogs that have domineering owners respond with counter-violence, either growling, snapping, or biting. If this describes your dog, you'll have a real problem when Bowser meets your child. If you continue these patterns, you will remain frustrated, perhaps resorting to more of the wrong kinds of "corrections," and leading the dog to failure.

Punishment, as domineering owners most often administer it, makes no sense to the dog. Behaviorally, punishment does have a role in some dogs' training, but it must be given at precisely the right moment, the right way, and for the right reasons. A dog that growls or snaps at his owner, for example, *should* be punished, but in many households that can be risky in itself. The dog will simply not tolerate corrections, or will react even more aggressively out of fear. If you don't trust your dog, you may need to call in a professional for guidance.

How does a dog get to that point in his relationship with the owner in the first place? What makes him decide to challenge you?

Punishment can cause the dog to fear what may be coming. Then, just when you need his attention most, he is too preoccupied with anxiety to function well. Such dogs usually end up avoiding their owners or trainers or trying to get away from them. Thus, commands such as heel, come, sit, and whoa are more likely to be ignored. This further frustrates such trainers, creating a never-ending circle of poorer and poorer performance. In time, such dogs can become biters. Often, their owners blame only the dog for whatever has gone wrong and may expect the trainer or behaviorist they contact to do something about it. They seem to want the dog's problem to become someone else's—someone they can blame for their own failure to communicate with the dog.

The domineering owner will have to change his ways for his dog to succeed with children. To adapt his dog well to a baby, such an owner will have to adopt a new strategy: taking charge through praise and whispers. Truly in-charge people never yell or use force. They don't need to.

The Overindulgent Owner

At the other extreme of the dog/owner relationship are the overindulgent owners. Such owners also can end up with dogs that do not "succeed" in family life. The dog has become

a substitute child to be fussed over excessively and incessantly, with the owner petting and cooing, thus acting and vocalizing in ways dogs interpret as subordinate or submissive. Even if you, personally, are not guilty of overindulging the dog, someone else in your household might be, and this alone can precipitate problems when introducing a baby.

Overindulgent owners often try to coax or bribe their dogs to obey, rather than simply expecting proper behavior. They may give in easily to what the dog wants, or walk away from the problem, thinking that by withdrawing their affections the dog will "learn" to behave. Instead, the dog only learns that he has succeeded in getting his own way. When the problems reach frustration level, the owner will try to use corrections, but such attempts usually do not last very long.

You are already headed toward problems if someone in your family pets your dog in ways that dogs interpret as submissive, or responds obediently whenever the dog barks or nudges to be petted, fed, or let in or out. If you share your bed with your dog, or do any number of other things the dog

19

interprets as submissive behavior, your dog will think it is his job to take charge.

Overindulgent owners generally try to avoid confrontations—even if the dog's behavior *needs* their attention. They will frequently try to cajole their dog, or reassure him. They will also say too much to their dog, confusing him in the process.

Overindulgent owners—particularly those who complain about destructive chewing—tend to give their dog a large selection of toys to chew, perhaps out of a feeling of guilt or a misplaced sense of parenting. Others have houses that are strewn with rawhide bones. (Not a good idea. They do not digest well and rawhide that has been around long enough to be coated with a black crud can harbor some pretty nasty bacteria.) They fail to recognize that giving the dog a wide variety of "chew toys" overemphasizes oral, or chewing, behavior, and makes it difficult for the dog to learn what he should *not* chew.

Some overindulgent owners even confess to "bribing" their dogs with numerous unearned treats throughout the day. Still others make a major production of saying "Good-bye" to the dog when they leave the house, or saying "Hello" when they return home, or confess to petting the dog effusively for no reason at all. In short, their dogs are coddled.

Many dogs become so spoiled they will not do their owners' bidding. Others become mean and nasty when their owners try to take charge. Dominance aggression and the guarding of food or training items are common behaviors in such dogs. Overindulgent owners often make excuses for the dog when anything goes wrong. They frequently blame themselves for everything the dog has done. As a result, his behavior problems are even more difficult to resolve.

If *anyone* in your family overindulges your dog, they must change this behavior before you bring a baby into the household. All family members should learn to communicate leadership and confidence in a humane manner that tells the dog they are in charge.

Other Owner Behaviors and Possible Outcomes

	Vacillating— Inconsistent when giving praise or corrections.	*This results in a dog that is as inconsistent as his owner.*
	Naive—Knows little about canine behavior. Will try anything/everything without regard to effectiveness.	*The dog, left to his own devices, will follow his instincts.*
	Insecure—May even fear the dog. Frequently says things like "My dog won't let me..."	*This owner's dog will be dominant, if not also aggressive.*
	Paranoid—Insists the dog is "trying to get even," or that he is vengeful in other ways.	*The dog will appear to be untrainable until exposed to proper leadership.*

Summary

As long as owners display even mild characteristics of either the dominant or overindulgent personality, their dogs may become a problem once a child enters the picture. If *both* types of owners are in contact with the same dog, there will be even more confusion. And, if both types of behavior are displayed by the same person—a mixture of punishment for some things and coddling or bribing for others—the dog will be even more confused and less able to learn successfully from that person.

Notice that we look to the owner, not the dog, for the reasons why the dog behaves in ways the owners do not like. The dog is the product of his relationship with the owner and with his daily environment.

Unless they change, neither the domineering nor the overindulgent dog owner is likely to succeed in getting the dog to adapt to a baby in the house. While the owners apply what they think works with people, the logic escapes the dog. He has an entirely different code of behavior. Interestingly, those parents who change their behaviors while working with the dog often find that the new behaviors work even more effectively with children.

A well-trained dog will investigate a child gently from a sitting position. Photo © Robert and Eunice Pearcy.

Bowser Learns How to Investigate Baby

Before you begin acclimating Bowser to the arrival of a new baby, or training him to accept a baby that is about to enter the "upright" stage (which is also a critical change for many dogs), you must be sure that you have established leadership over Bowser. He should also know the basic obedience commands described in Part II of this book. Then you can begin teaching him how to safely investigate the baby and the baby's furnishings. When possible, all adults in the household should participate in this training.

You'll need a receiving blanket, a doll, a stroller, and a few other items that you plan to use around the baby. Begin these exercises several months in advance of the baby's expected arrival.

The parents should take turns holding a receiving blanket as though it were wrapped around an infant. Allow Bowser to investigate thoroughly. You want to get both your scent and his on the item. It's perfectly sanitary. You'll launder the items periodically anyhow, but dogs can smell in parts per billion so the blanket will always have a familiar scent to the dog.

Once Bowser is accustomed to the articles, wrap one of the receiving blankets around a stuffed animal or doll, but *not* around one of Bowser's dog toys. Carry it around on occasion. If Father feels a bit silly, he should look upon it not as playing with dolls, but as behavioral conditioning that will help Bowser adapt to a child.

In calm surroundings, sit on a sofa or chair holding the doll. Allow the dog to investigate, but insist that he keep all four feet on the ground at all times. The best approach is to have Bowser sit or lie down before introducing the new doll. With more of his body on the floor it is more difficult for him to investigate aggressively. If you have not already taught the sit command, do so now. Then, with just a little extra effort with the doll, you can teach your dog to sit whenever the baby is placed anywhere near him.

Next, lay your doll down, give the "Easy" command, and allow Bowser to sniff the doll to satisfy his curiosity. Once he gets used to doing this with a doll, he will have less curiosity when your baby arrives. Your attitude and tone are important in everything you do. Bowser will learn to copy your behavior in many situations, so be sure you set a calm example around the doll. You can help by talking soothingly to the doll on occasion.

Never pull the doll away or hold it high overhead while Bowser is investigating. He might try to reach for it with his teeth. If he starts doing that he may think he's being invited to grab the "baby" for a game

24

of tug-of-war. This could lead to a biting response whenever the baby is taken from his reach.

Instead, if Bowser tries to use his teeth, say "Leave it" in firm, clipped voice tones. If necessary, clamp his muzzle closed with your thumb over the top and your fingers in the "V" formed by the bones under his chin.

Any time you must correct Bowser, *lay the doll down first.* One owner tried to make the correction by hitting the dog in the head with the doll. When asked why, she said, "Well, it certainly can't hurt him, it's soft enough." Then she realized that she had, in effect, just hit the dog over the head with her new baby and cringed at what that one thoughtless moment might have set up in her dog's mind.

Even if Bowser behaves immediately after you correct him, you should set the doll down and have him do a couple of heels and sits to earn your praise. Otherwise he could be confused and think you praised him for his misbehavior rather than for turning his head away from the doll. End the training for a while and repeat it again later.

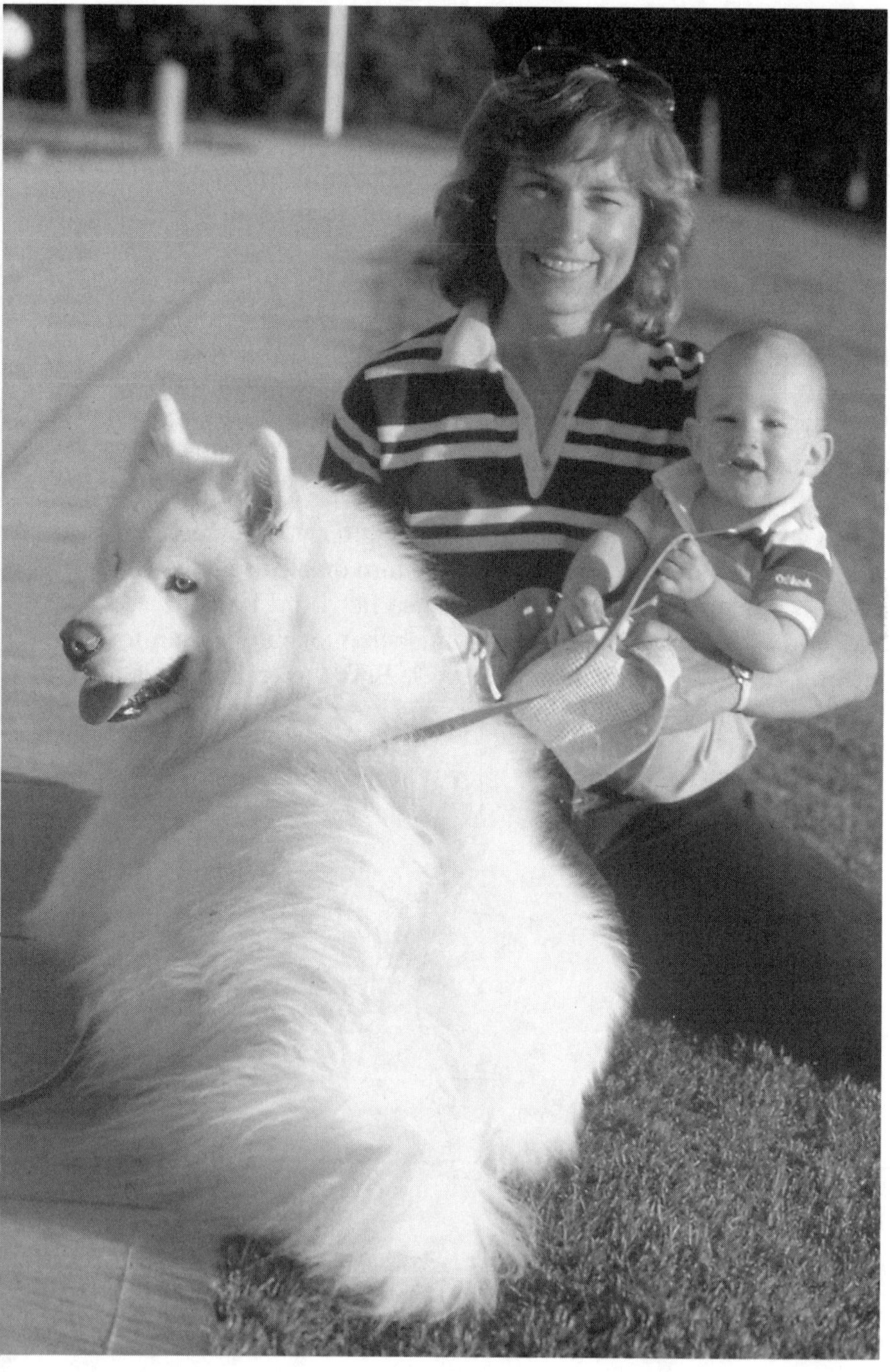

Photo © Kent and Donna Dannen.

Bowser Learns to Walk with Baby

As soon as you can, start to introduce Bowser to the baby carriage or stroller. If you plan to have Bowser walk with you and the new baby, he will have to know how to walk quietly on a leash without straining.

Obedience school is helpful when training this exercise, but if you are unable to attend a class you can train at home. Put your dog on a ten-foot leash and collar. Start out in your backyard. Go to one place and stand there. If Bowser tries to dart away, you should turn and anchor down. Allow the leash to cross your hip to absorb the impact when he reaches the end of the leash. Say nothing. He will assume the restraint occurred because he tried to run off—not because you corrected him.

As he returns to you, say "There you are. Good heel," in a very pleasant voice and keep on walking. He will come to learn that near you is the best place to be. Continue to move to different spots in the yard and wait there until he starts to dash away. When he does, face the opposite direction, causing him to correct himself each time.

At this stage, your dog may decide to lag behind where he can keep a better eye on what you might do next. When that happens, do a complete about turn, taking the leash tension on your hips, and walk directly toward your dog. As you do, he will move toward your rear to ease the slack. When you pass him, he will have to move up to your side to relieve the pressure again. Keep walking and, after a few steps, say "What a good heel."

Once he is paying close attention to you and staying at your side, you can begin the basics of heeling. Simply walk at least twenty feet from one place to another in the yard. He should stay with you now. The leash should be completely slack. If he forges ahead, turn sharply in the opposite direction, give the lead even more slack, and when he reaches the end of the lead, say nothing. As he catches up with you, this time say "Good heel" in long, reassuring tones. Repeat this until he is at your side each time you do an about turn.

Next, start making right turns in the same manner. Allow Bowser to make his own corrections until he no longer drifts away when you turn. Then start making left turns.

To make left turns, take the slack out of the leash as you are heeling, but do not pull the lead tight. Time your turn so that you can step in front of the dog's chest with your foot. Just make sure you do not walk into his side. Say nothing. After a few of these "close calls," Bowser will be ready to pivot before you cut in front of him.

Now you can start leading him along as you push the carriage or stroller. Make sure he walks calmly without interfering with the baby carriage, dragging you to a stop, or pulling you in a different direction. When you stop, he should sit or stand quietly. Place the doll in the carriage and bend over to check on it periodically. Bowser should not interfere or try to distract your attention away from the "baby."

You can introduce other baby items, such as a changing table, car seat, swing, or crib in much the same way. It will be easier for Bowser if the furniture and equipment you plan to use around the baby is in place and familiar before baby comes home. But don't let Bowser think it belongs to him or let him become possessive of any place or item. Remember, he must have his own bed and his own "safe place" away from the baby or child's area.

Bowser Learns That Babies Cry

Another important step before the baby comes home is to get Bowser used to a baby's cry. A dog can mistake a baby's cry for a wounded animal's cry. A dog can also mistake an infant thrashing helplessly about for the motions of a wounded animal. Since dogs in the wild will generally put a sick or wounded animal out of its misery, you can see the potential problem.

Your goal should be to have Bowser come to you whenever the baby cries. Then you will "investigate," take care of the situation, and thank the dog. Bowser needs to learn that a

WA-A-H!

baby's cry is something you will take care of and, after he has notified you, it is not his concern.

Conditioning your dog to a baby crying before your child is born may sound impractical, but it need not be. Make a tape recording of several versions of an infant's cry with about 30 seconds of silence at the start and 10 to 15 seconds of silence in between. You can ask the hospital for permission to record babies crying in the nursery where you plan to have your baby.

Place the recorder in the crib or playpen when Bowser is not watching. Then make a big show of putting the doll in, and let Bowser see you do it. As you lay the doll down, flip on the player's switch and walk away. Have Bowser on a six-foot or ten-foot lead and collar well beforehand.

As the tape starts playing the infant's cries, pick up the leash, tell Bowser to "Come," and draw him toward you out of the room. Praise him just as the crying stops, then let him go.

With each successive cry, Bowser may want to go back and investigate. Allow him to approach the area, but only with all

four feet on the ground. Then, at once, command "Come" again and draw him toward you out of the room. Praise him for coming and always take the pressure off the leash as soon as he starts moving toward you. If he tries to head back into the room before the next cry, call him and draw him to you again. Praise him for coming.

You are teaching the dog it is okay to investigate the sound of a baby's cry with all four feet on the ground, but then he must come to you immediately and you will take care of it. After a few brief sessions, once the dog is coming reliably, return to the room with the dog, reach down and shut off the recorder as you pick up the "baby," and thank your dog.

In later sessions, you should only pick up the "baby" once in a while. Gradually increase the distance of the come until Bowser will come to you wherever you are in the house when he hears the baby's cry. Each time, accompany the dog back to the baby, tell him to "Sit," shut off the recorder, say "Thank you" to him, and pat him on top of the head. Say "Good dog" in a soothing voice and walk the dog out of the room.

A good training schedule would be to conduct two or three sessions, fifteen minutes long, in the morning and then give him at least a two-hour break. Do two or three more sessions in the afternoon. Occasionally, add a session late at night.

Soon Bowser will be accustomed to the baby's cry—and you'll be conditioned for getting up in the middle of the night after the baby arrives.

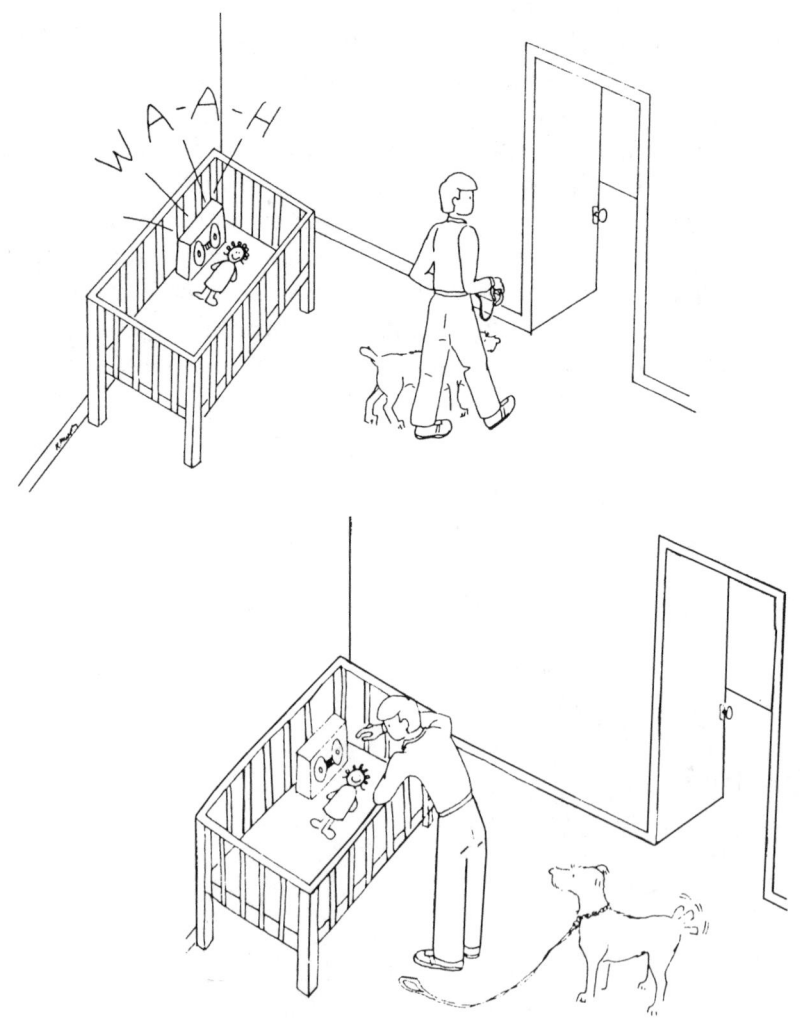

Welcoming Baby

After your baby is born, but is still in the hospital, have someone bring home an item of clothing or a receiving blanket that has surrounded the baby. Ask Bowser to sit. Release him from the sit and then allow him to sniff the baby's clothing. If he tries to mouth the item, take it away. Gradually, teach the dog that the presence of anything that contains the baby's scent is his cue to remain calm and quiet.

When you bring the baby home, have someone else carry the baby. Mother should enter the house first, without the baby,

and should greet the dog affectionately. Once the greeting is over and the dog is calm, introduce additional items that have the baby's fresh scent. Ask Bowser to sit and, when he obeys, allow him to sniff the items. Only then should someone bring the baby into the room. Avoid making the baby the center of attention, which will cause the dog to feel rejected, or making the dog struggle to be petted when you're handling the baby. This will help to prevent the dog from competing for attention.

For the next few weeks both owners should give the dog some extra attention to allay any "sibling rivalry." From now on, remember to give the dog some personal time with you each day. Try not to allow the baby to interfere with Bowser's regular activities with you—feeding, grooming, walks, exercise, and play time.

Make Baby a Safe Place

In the early sessions with the baby, periodically have someone else hold the baby while Mom pets Bowser—but only pet him when he remains calm. This begins the basic association that Bowser has nice things happen when he is around the baby. If he misbehaves mildly it is better to distract him rather than to correct him at first. Put more effort into encouraging the dog's good behavior. Strive to have only *positive* experiences whenever the dog is around the baby.

At times, when Bowser is calm near the baby, give him a small treat. This will further reinforce his belief that being calm around the baby earns rewards. It just may be true that a dog's heart is reached through his stomach. Certainly, Bowser likes his treats, and they are a great motivator of performance when given correctly. Be careful not to overdo the treats, however, or Bowser will come to expect them whenever the baby is near. And never bribe the dog in advance in hopes that he will behave. An unearned treat may convince him that there is no need to obey, or it may actually reinforce

disobedience. If nothing else, it is a lost opportunity to teach the dog that he has to *earn* the good things you offer.

In subsequent sessions, let various people, including Mom, hold the baby when Bowser is brought into the room. The treats can be given less frequently now. Gradually, Bowser will come to have a mild, pleasant association with the baby. You don't want him to become so excited that he creates a disturbance whenever the baby is in the room with him. Neither do you want Bowser to feel that he might be punished or scolded when the baby is near.

 Bringing a new toddler into Bowser's household? Most techniques in this book can be modified and used to introduce adopted children, grandchildren, or children belonging to a new spouse. Refer to the section on toddlers and the modify the training accordingly.

Use a Screen Door to Isolate the Baby

If you want to keep Bowser out of the baby's room temporarily, you can mount a screen door in the bedroom doorway. Be sure to put a scratch-proof panel across the bottom. Never chase Bowser from the room when closing the door, and make sure your voice tones are always friendly when you guide him out of the room. Leave no opportunity for misinterpretation. Never give Bowser a reason to associate unpleasantness with the baby.

Shhhh. Baby's Sleeping

Within the first few days after baby's home-coming, while the baby is asleep and Bowser is present, look at Bowser and softly say, "Shhhh, Baby's sleeping." Then praise him if he remains calm. This gives you another command to work with and encourages Bowser's calmness through praise.

Never use the command if he is acting up or barking—at least not in the early stages. If he disobeys even once and gets away with it, the command will lose its effectiveness. Instead, if he acts up when the baby is asleep, either put him outside or ignore him.

When Baby Cries

It is one thing to condition Bowser to a tape recording of a baby crying: It is quite another for new Mothers to remain calm when the real baby cries. The key to success here—for mother, child, and Bowser—is that a calm reaction will lead to a calmer household for everyone, even in an emergency.

If the baby screams, remember that it takes about 3.2 seconds to get to the baby's room from any part of the average house at a brisk walk. A mad dash could take hours—including the trip to the hospital (after stumbling over a chair, a rug, Bowser, and so on)—especially if Bowser copies your behavior and starts running, too. Furthermore, if you run and cause Bowser to run toward the baby, you could trigger an instinct in the dog that begins with chasing and ends with biting. Not a good idea. Remember what we said earlier: Dogs sometimes mistake a baby's crying for a wounded animal.

Walk calmly to the bedroom and you will build the basis for several other successes in the future.

Safeguarding Baby

Once at home, your baby should always be kept at a higher level than the dog. Playpens, highchairs, and cribs are ideal. Unless you are right in the room with the baby next to you, *do not* leave the baby and the dog on the floor together. Dogs "correct" subordinates or puppies with their mouths, so it would be perfectly logical for your dog to bite your baby's face or neck if the child did something the dog did not like.

A dog can also mistake an infant for a toy to be taken and played with. Bowser might even try to carry the baby off out of a misplaced sense of protectiveness. Naturally, these situations should not be allowed, since in both cases the dog will bite the baby. Remember, dogs do not need to be vicious to bite.

When Baby Is Eating

Many accidental injuries occur when either
the baby or the dog are eating and the other tries
to share. As soon as your child reaches the baby-
food stage, teach Bowser to remain calmly in the
room with you when you feed the baby. This is much better
than forcing him to stay out of the room at feeding time, which
again can lead to anxiety and jealousy. Make sure the dog does
not pester for food. He should either sit or lie down while you
feed the baby.

Periodically, after baby has eaten, feed Bowser the slight
remains. You can do this with part of a biscuit as well. This will
put the baby's saliva on the food before the dog eats, which further encourages subordinate behaviors in the dog.

Teach Bowser Not to Guard His Food

For safety, you should condition Bowser to having his food removed, his dish taken away, or someone placing their hand in the dish without the dog becoming upset. *The procedures described are designed to help prevent accidents, rather than to allow your child to interfere with Bowser's meals.* Children should always be taught to leave a dog alone when he is eating or sleeping.

If you feed Bowser according to the simple procedure outlined in Rapport Skills™ in Part II of this book, you should make rapid progress with this exercise. At his regular feeding time, call Bowser to you and require him to perform a sit or a down before giving him his food. (This assumes he knows the commands by now.)

If he barks insistently, or otherwise refuses to perform the command, take his food away. He may have to go one or two days without eating in order to learn that demanding or refusing to obey goes unrewarded. (In tests, dogs have gone almost two weeks without eating with no adverse effects.) Be sure the

dog has fresh water at all times, however. If you are worried about nutrition, you can give him a multi-vitamin tablet.

Once Bowser performs the command, hold his food dish at his

eye level until he starts eating. If he growls or jumps up, take it away. If he remains calm, gradually lower the dish to the floor and walk away. Over several feedings, increase the amount of time you stand near his dish before walking away. Praise him each time he remains calm. Set your daily goals low enough that he is not tempted to misbehave. (You can feed half-rations twice a day to move this training along faster.)

After several days, you should be able to hold the dish for two minutes before giving it to him, then stand near him for at least two minutes as he eats. When Bowser has reached this level in earning his dinner, start conditioning him with an occasional dog biscuit or small treat in his bowl. Break the biscuit into several small pieces, or have several small treats available, before you call him to his bowl. Kneel on one knee, placing the bowl between you and the dog. The front of your body should face away from the bowl and the dog.

As he comes to you, remain crouched, say "Good come," and put one piece of the treat into the bowl. Allow Bowser to eat it. If he remains calm, continue to feed him one piece at a time. When it is gone, say "All gone," and praise him again as you rise and walk away. You are further conditioning him to the fact that all good things come from you. He is also learning that "All gone" means "It's over, that's it. No more." And both are being accomplished in a safe, humane way.

If your dog tries to nudge your hand or jump on you to get the rest of the pieces, say "All gone," and simply walk to the counter and put the treats away. Let him know by your "cold shoulder" attitude that he just lost his chance for the rest of the treat. You do not need to scold. Continue this procedure twice a day for three or four days. This is desensitizing him to having the baby approach his food dish later.

The next step takes place at mealtime: Put two ounces of food in his dish and call him. Stand within fifteen feet, but not too close. When he finishes this morsel and looks for more, ask, "More?" If he shows calm enthusiasm, give him two ounces more and stand a bit closer to him as he eats. If he misbehaves, say "All gone," and walk away. That ends his dinner. Because of previous conditioning, he will get the message.

When you can feed Bowser readily and you can remain standing twelve or fifteen feet away, you should repeat the procedure starting at ten feet away and gradually closing the distance to about five feet over three or four days. Praise Bowser for calm behavior; end the meal and say "All gone" whenever he misbehaves.

The big test comes next. Stand at his bowl, with his meal in another dish on a nearby counter or table. Call Bowser to you and give him the first two ounces as you stand right beside his bowl. If he misbehaves, he gets no more food. If he behaves, ask "More?" and then change the procedure. With the friendliest attitude possible, pick up his bowl and, if he behaves, reward him by adding another two ounces at counter level before returning the bowl to him. Continue this for several days, responding to his behavior as discussed previously.

By now Bowser understands that you are the source of food, and that he is frequently "rewarded" (with more food and praise).

Now you can begin the ultimate test. Allow him to go twenty-four hours without any food at all. Prepare his dinner, then call him to you. Present the entire meal to him at eye level and hold it there until he has eaten half of it. Then lower the bowl to the floor, crouching down as you do so. Even though the food is in front of him, ask him if he wants "More?" Then, pick up the bowl and set it on the counter.

Since he is conditioned that "More" means good things to come, he should remain calm. If so, pick up the bowl of food again and give him the rest of his meal, praising him for remaining calm. If he misbehaves, say "Enough" in the sternest voice possible, then walk away. Do not let him have the rest of the meal. By now, Bowser has had sufficient opportunity to learn what you expect from him. He should no longer challenge that, and should respect your verbal assertions by backing down. If not, you should seek professional help for him.

"Enough" should sound like "RRRUFF," which comes close to the vocalization a dog would make to verbally back down another dog.

Follow those steps for several days to make sure Bowser learns that good behavior enables him to eat, and bad behavior causes him to miss the rest of his meal. Test what you have achieved over the next several days by walking to and from him, picking up his dish, and setting it down. Do this for at least ten meals before you allow the baby in the room while Bowser is eating.

The last step is to give Bowser his dinner and periodically reach in and take out a handful of food, then put it back. If you use moist food, do it anyway. Hands wash easily. This will get Bowser used to having his food taken away, just in case the baby should reach into his bowl. As stated earlier, this procedure is only meant to desensitize Bowser in case the baby should decide to reach into the bowl or take a piece of food from the floor. As a matter of safe practice, keep the baby away from Bowser's food bowl when he is eating.

When you have worked through this entire procedure at least ten times, gradually introduce the baby into the room while Bowser is eating. When you begin, first bring the baby into the room and then put Bowser's food down. This will help him learn that the presence of the baby means good things. Keep the baby off the floor and away from the dish. When Bowser has stopped eating, whether or not he has cleaned up his bowl, remove the dish from the floor and put it out of reach until the next meal.

When toddlers start to crawl, let caution be your watchword. Photo © Kent and Donna Dannen.

When Baby Starts to Crawl

Before you start putting the child on the floor, be certain that the relationship with Bowser will proceed smoothly. Let caution be your watchword.

First you want to ensure that your dog does not react aggressively to fast-moving objects or shrill noises. If he does, you should either have a professional help you desensitize your dog, or consider getting rid of him. Otherwise, if your child moves quickly or screeches with excitement, the dog could respond by chasing and biting—natural reflexes in many dogs.

If your dog has no reactions to fast-moving objects or shrill sounds, you can proceed to the next step. Clip a leash onto Bowser's collar and allow him to enter a room where you are sitting on the sofa or a chair with the child. When the dog is calm, have a helper pick up the end of his leash as you ease yourself and the baby down to the floor. Allow Bowser to "investigate." Praise him if he remains calm. If he shows any sign of aggression, protect your baby's face and your own and have your helper take the dog out of the room immediately. You should get professional help with this dog.

If all goes well (and it should since you would not attempt this with a dog that has problems), have your helper take the dog from the room and put the baby in a crib or playpen. Go back and pet the dog. Repeat the process several times over several days—but not more than three times within fifteen minutes without at least an hour's break in between. If the dog continues to behave well, begin moving yourself a little farther away from the baby each time the dog is brought in.

The baby's activity level will increase rapidly after this stage. He may begin to reach for the dog, crawl over him, pull his ears or tail, or pinch his feet. An intended pat can look more like a well-aimed slap from the dog's point of view. Never leave a dog and a crawling baby alone together. Although most dogs seem to enjoy toddlers and want to snuggle with them or lick their faces, even the best mannered dog can react aggressively when startled or hurt. Don't expect either the baby or Bowser to "know better" than to inflict unintended injury to the other.

Never leave a dog and a crawling baby alone together. Photo © Kent and Donna Dannen.

During this stage of your baby's development, he or she and Bowser will most likely begin to bond. This could lead to Bowser becoming more protective of the child. Try to prevent any overprotective behavior, but allow good times together. Playing in the yard, going for a walk in the park, sharing family time together on the floor, and even allowing Baby to lie beside Bowser on the floor or explore his toes, coat, and ears, all build memorable moments of shared love and companionship.

Countless stories have been told of dogs pulling a baby from danger or protecting them with their lives. Other stories,

Baby-Proof Bowser's Belongings

When Baby begins crawling, you will naturally want to remove objects that might break, cover electrical outlets, and take other safety precautions around the house. Include Bowser in this safety routine, too. Make sure the dog's toys, food dish, and chewies are not within the baby's reach. Move Bowser's bed to a room where the baby is not allowed, or a corner that Baby can't easily get into. Do not let Bowser's crate or bed become a play area for Baby. Give Bowser his own toys and make sure that he learns *not* to play with the baby's belongings.

perhaps not so easily recounted, can be told of babies having their faces maimed, being pushed over by an excited dog and suffering broken bones, or just having an unfortunate incident frighten them so badly that they are forever afraid of dogs. While you may trust your dog and enjoy seeing the companionship that is developing, remember not to be so trusting that you allow Baby and Bowser together unsupervised. That time should not come until much later.

When Bowser "Guards"

The first signs of "guarding" behavior around the baby may occur near Bowser's food dish. Dogs are sometimes overprotective of their food, even around adults, so it is little wonder that they defend it when children venture near. If the dog growls at the owners when they approach the dog while he is eating, this indicates a lack of owner leadership and could pose a real threat to the child.

The key is to build that rapport first before the baby arrives. The dog will learn that since you are in charge, he does not have to be. If you followed the advice offered in other chapters, you should succeed. If your child is already a toddler, you can still succeed by taking Bowser through all of the steps described—especially the feeding procedure. Keep in mind that it will be more difficult to teach a dog not to guard if he has already learned to get away with "guarding" food or possessions around adult members of the household.

Even if food guarding is not a problem, keep the child's toys away from the dog, and give the dog only one toy of his own, preferably a nylon chew bone. This will help him to learn what he is allowed to chew. Keep the child away from Bowser's toy. This will help to avoid any competitive situations.

When Bowser Overprotects

An overprotective dog may be convinced that his owners are incapable of providing the needed protection. This message is transmitted to the dog through a series of subtle cues. Gestures, voice tones, and proper use of physical contact are the clearest ways to communicate with a dog. The Rapport Skills™ exercises, carried out long before baby arrives and continued throughout Bowser's life, provide the best answer.

If you encourage Bowser to be *too* protective of the baby, he may enjoy the job so much that he even growls at the adults in the family. Always teach Bowser that his job is to sound the alert and then let you take over.

Baby's Bed
Is Not Bowser's Den

As the rapport builds between the baby and the dog, do not be tempted to allow Bowser to sleep with the child, say at the foot of the bed. Your child's bed is not the dog's den. Sharing a bed may give Bowser a false sense of equal status with the child when you should be encouraging him to be subordinate to the baby.

If you want to permit Bowser to be with your child at night, start by leashing him to the foot of the bed in a way that keeps him from sidling up on the bed during the night. Soon he will adjust to this position—below the child. This will encourage further positive bonding between the child and Bowser—especially if the dog is still young.

What Not to Do
When Bowser Misbehaves

If you need to stop your dog from misbe-
having, direct punishment is rarely as effective
as distracting him from whatever he is doing, or
about to do. Keep in mind that physical punishment
does very little to correct problem behavior in dogs. Soon the
dog learns to misbehave only when he cannot be punished. If
guarding food or possessions is the problem, you can see how
this might lead to a child being bitten.

Physical punishment can actually worsen or intensify an
undesirable behavior. It may also cause the dog to redirect his
aggression elsewhere, or even attack the person who metes out
the punishment. One can never generalize for all breeds, ages,
learning abilities, training skills, and family situations. However,
punishment is clearly the least effective way to train.

*Toddlers
must learn
how to
stroke a
dog gently.
Photo ©
Robert and
Eunice
Pearcy.*

Groups like this could easily frighten or agitate some dogs. Photo © Click the Photo Connection.

Toddlers and Dogs

When Baby becomes a toddler, Bowser's relationship is likely to change. As the child begins to stand upright, the dog senses that the baby is going through another stage. Suddenly the child who could "get away with anything" may be challenged with growls, aggressive postures, or even mouthing and nipping. This, of course, should not be tolerated, although it is natural for the dog to behave this way in the absence of human leadership and supervision.

While the baby is still a growing infant, take Bowser, alone, to parks or school yards where he can see children playing at a distance. Practice his obedience commands there so that he will learn that you are in charge when children are present and that you expect good behavior from him. Do everything possible to help Bowser succeed in these surroundings. Be sure to praise him for calm behavior.

If possible, introduce toddlers into the home, gradually, before your child reaches the walking stage. Some dogs may try to mount toddlers. This behavior is a perfectly normal way for the dog to show dominance and has no sexual connotation. To anticipate this, have him on a leash and collar. Then, if Bowser tries to mount, say "Off," and tighten the leash so no contact is made. Heel the dog away. Continue this until he will sit at your command in a child's presence.

Supervise. Expect obedience. Praise calmness.

Never Alone

This bears repeating: Never leave your dog alone in the room with a young child. Too many unpredictable things could happen, and dogs become less patient when toddlers do things they may have gotten away with at an earlier stage. If you were not in the room, the dog might try to give a well-meaning "correction" to the toddler who pulls his ear or tail. Unfortunately, dogs naturally use their mouths and teeth to do this. Even friendly pawing could cause serious injury.

As your child begins to walk, the dog could accidentally bump into the baby and knock him or her into a piece of sharp furniture or something even more damaging. Take precautions

---

 Teach Baby How to Treat Bowser

 When Baby starts to walk, you begin teaching the words "No" and "Leave it alone." This is also the time to begin teaching the baby how to behave around Bowser.

- Sit on the floor when petting the dog.
- Do not go near the dog when he is eating.
- Extend a hand, palm down, for the dog to sniff before reaching for him.

- Don't startle a dog when he is sleeping.

- Do not pick up or carry a dog or puppy (until the child is much older and has learned how to hold the dog).

- Do not put things in the dog's ears, eyes or mouth.

and stay in the room when children and dogs are together on the floor.

Rarely does a dog instigate the problems that occur between Baby and Bowser. Most problems are the result of unsupervised contact or allowing the baby to harrass the dog. If you're there, you can head off the problem. If you're not, you may never know why your dog "attacked" your child. Praise the child for behaving properly, but redirect his or her attention when you anticipate an impending problem. Don't wait for a disaster and then yell. Prevent the situation by keeping a close eye on the child whenever Bowser is around.

Children should sit on the floor to pet a dog. Never leave a baby and a dog alone together. Photo © Jan Whitaker.

Hand-feeding a dog, under adult supervision, can help a child establish a proper rapport between the two. Photo © Kent and Donna Dannen.

Fringe Benefits

One of the side benefits of this training and conditioning is that your dog will obey you better everywhere. The communications skills this book covers will let Bowser know you are a calm, dependable leader. From his viewpoint, you are the "top dog." He will have learned that all good things come from following your good advice.

As the child moves through the toddler stage, continue the walks and the Rapport Skills™ exercises with Bowser. Have him perform obedience commands periodically before petting him or feeding him. Once Bowser knows the rules, it is easy to reinforce them through repetition and praise. Now you can begin to have your child present as you run through the Rapport Skills™. In fact, allow him to perform the skills under your supervision, as soon as he or she is able.

Your outcome? Bowser will have a sense of place, of responsibility, of belonging. Your entire family will benefit.

This dog is visiting a kindergarten class—another good way to socialize your dog when he is properly trained and also teach children about the responsibilities of owning a dog. Photo © Robert and Eunice Pearcy.

Bowser as Victim

We have considered what might happen to the child. What about Bowser? Children under five have been caught kicking dogs, poking sharp items in their eyes and noses, pulling their tails, and trying to hit them with various tools like hammers and screwdrivers. Incredible as it may seem, there have even been reports of children pouring irritating fluids and cleansers on dogs, dumping hot liquid on them, burning them with a parent's cigarette, and worse.

 As early as possible, teach the child what the dog needs:

- Quiet places to sleep, eat and rest
- Gentle petting and no hitting, pinching, or pulling
- Calm voice tones
- No running

Children must learn not to strike, pinch, or pull a dog's ears or skin.
Photo © Robert and Eunice Pearcy.

Wait until your child is old enough to help with care and training before getting him or her a puppy. Photo © Jan Whitaker.

Don't Get a Dog "for Baby"

If you already have a dog in your household when your child is born, this book will help you make the best of the situation. If you don't, it is never a good idea to acquire a dog because you think your toddler needs a companion. Don't bring a new dog into the household of a family if your child is too young to participate in some of the care and feeding.

Even then, it is unwise to bring a new dog into the household unless the child clearly wants a dog. If the child resents having to help take care of the dog, has a fear of dogs, or simply does not want a dog, unfortunate situations could arise.

Finally, no child under the age of ten years, at least, has enough maturity to take total responsibility for a dog—no exceptions. An adult must be willing to take on the job and oversee the child's limited role in the dog's care.

Even in families with older children, it may be unrealistic to expect the children to shoulder the entire responsibility. They are just learning how to handle school schedules, sports, music lessons, and other activities, juggle household obligations, and deal with the growing complexity of relationships with others their own age.

When children are involved at an appropriate level, the relationship between them and the dog can be more positive. However, the experience needs to be pleasant for them—not a chore that they resent. Caring for Bowser can be an opportunity for all of you to socialize. Depending upon the child's age, he or she can help with feeding the dog, bathing him, brushing him, playing ball with him, and so on.

A PUPPY for Your Child?

- Don't buy a puppy for a baby so they can "grow up together." You'll have your hands full with just the baby until he is past the toddler stage.

- Wait until the child is old enough to learn to handle a puppy with care.

- It is best if the child can participate in some of the dog's care, even if only minimally. Toddlers love to participate in bathing the dog, especially in summer.

- If the dog is to be truly the child's pet, then the child should be old enough to feed, water, and brush the puppy. If the dog is to be a family pet, either everyone can share or the parents should plan to assume all responsibilities. The child must not resent the pet.

- Make sure the child, not you, wants the puppy, and that he or she participates in the selection, preparation, and daily routine.

- Don't get a breed of dog that is too delicate for the youngster to handle safely.

- Don't select a puppy or dog that is too rowdy or rough for your child.

- Make sure you observe the temperament and personality of the puppy's mother. If she is aggressive or excessively shy, find another puppy.

- Consider an older dog only if he has been raised or properly socialized with children.

Photo © Click the Photo Connection.

A Word About Dogs That Bite

A dog that bites family members is unsafe around children. Any bite should cause serious concern and a dog that bites is a risk around babies. Harsh as it may seem, there should be no second chances when babies are involved—regardless of why the dog may have bitten.

Some dogs bite because they are dominant and try to control things with their mouths. Dominant dogs that bite are often out of the owners' control and "won't listen." They will frequently inflict one puncture wound and may either hang on or release once they have bitten.

In contrast, a fear-biter believes he needs to bite to protect himself and uses his teeth when he is afraid. Frequently, a fear-biter will thrash and shred as he bites.

We have already discussed the prey-chasing, prey-killing instinct in dogs. Dogs with this form of aggression frequently nip at anything that moves, attempt to bring it down, and—in the extreme—kill it. Dogs that chase (and might kill) squirrels, rabbits or other "prey," including cats, can be risky to have around young children. Never allow your dog to chase or catch anything if you plan to raise children around him.

Other dogs may nip or "mouth" children to "correct" them—usually indicating that the dog does not perceive that family is in charge within the household.

Still others bite as a response to pain when a child hurts the dog. Although it may not be the dog's "fault" in this situation, the child is likely to repeat the behavior and the dog is likely to repeat the response—resulting in another bite. When a dog bites as a reaction to pain, it is likely that no adult was supervising while the dog and baby were together. Perhaps that situation, too, may occur again.

The fact remains: For the child's safety, and possibly the dog's, the dog that bites should not be kept in this household.

Older children like to play "chase" with a dog. Prevent this if there's a toddler in the house. Photo © Judith Strom.

PART II

BOWSER'S BASIC TRAINING

Modify behavior, teach manners, and resolve problems

Who's in Charge?

Bob's dog barks to be let out. Janet's dog nudges her to be petted or fed. Frank's dog growls whenever someone comes near his food bowl or the crate where he sleeps. Dale's dog barks aggressively when anyone enters the house. Theresa's dog put a gash in her face that required one hundred and fifty stitches to close after she tried to get him away from the roast on the kitchen table.

Do these problems sound unrelated? Surprisingly, they all stem from the same common cause—a misplaced sense of dominance. Many trainers, behaviorists, and ethnologists consider dominance to be the major contributing factor in many types of problems between dogs and their owners.

The Dog as Part of a Pack

Despite domestication, dogs still share much in common with their wolf ancestors—their society always needs a leader. Like wolves, dogs are pack animals and they have a pecking order, just as chickens—and even humans—do. Among dogs, as in many other species, the drive to dominate is more likely to occur in males than in females, nonetheless it can occur in either sex. If dogs could speak, they'd likely quote a famous statesman who put it this way: "Either lead, follow, or get out of the way."

In some breeds of dogs the drive to rise to the top of the ranks—to dominate—is stronger than in others. A Bassett Hound is not going to be as assertive, for example, as an Akita when it comes to striving for control over the pack. In fact, within the same *breed*, some dogs will be more dominant than others due to genetics or the way they were raised.

Wolves and dogs still have more than sixty behaviors in common, as noted by J. P. Scott, Ph.D., and they use approximately a dozen of these to establish and maintain a social order. Because of their domestication, dogs will respond to human approximations of these signals in much the same way as they would to another dog that displayed the "real thing."

We are successful in raising our dogs primarily because *our dogs have learned to adapt to us*—not the other way around. Most dogs adapt well; a few get out of control because of the way the owners interact with them. Despite domestication, dogs will still do what comes naturally for them. They don't think the same way we do, and they interpret voice and body language the way their own species does, not the way we humans do.

Children and puppies can bond well when adults properly supervise them.
Photo © Robert and Eunice Pearcy.

Controlling Behavior with Rapport Skills™

In the past, owners were told that the best way to deal with a dominant dog was to use either obedience training or punishment. Yet, as important as it is to train dogs to respond to basic commands such as sit, down, and come, owners of dominant dogs can be bitten if they try to "correct" a dog's refusal to obey such commands. Also, obedience training does not deal with problems that stem from a dog's dominance. Punishment is even worse. Dominant dogs often retaliate when owners try to punish them.

There is a better way; namely, to take charge by using human approximations of the same signals both dogs and wolves use to establish or maintain their status within the pack. I call these Rapport Skills™. These concepts have been endorsed by Dr. J. P. Scott, a pioneer in this field who also contributed to their development. [Scott is a co-author of the seminal book *Genetics and the Social Behavior of the Dog* (John P. Scott and John L. Fuller, University of Chicago Press, 1998).]

The skills are arranged in sequence. They start with the one the dog is least likely to resist and gradually move toward the ones a dominant dog is more likely to resist. Do not advance to a new one until the dog has totally accepted all the previous ones. As you move forward, continue to maintain *all* the ones your dog now accepts. If your dog has been even mildly aggressive toward people, consult a qualified canine behaviorist before undertaking this program.

Sleeping Habits

Make sure your dog has at least one "safe" place, such as a favorite corner of a room. When he is there, he must be free from all punishment or reprimands. "People" furniture does not make a good "safe place" if you want to establish better control over your dog, however. From now on, never allow him to sleep on the bed with you. Doing so gives him signals that he has a higher status in the pack than he should have. To a dog, one bed is as good as another. Be sure he has his own.

Eating Habits

Control is a key issue with dominant dogs, and food provides the best way to initiate it. At feeding time, put your dog in another room and close the door. Have someone open the door as you call "(Name), Here." When he comes, say "Good here" and immediately offer him a few pellets of dry food directly from your open hand. If he refuses to eat from your hand, or does *anything* else, say nothing. Don't feed him. Instead, ignore him and walk away. Repeat the process in ten minutes. If he fails again to eat from your hand, remain still and say "All right" to release him. Try one more time an hour later. If he fails again, do not feed him anything until the next day. Keep fresh water down for him, however. Some dogs may take three or four days before they will go through this ritual successfully, but they will not starve. After all, your request is a reasonable one, and his refusal or obedience is entirely under his control—so far.

When he accepts food from your hand, say "All right." Set his dinner bowl down and quietly stand upright beside the bowl as he eats the rest of the meal. If he walks at least fifteen feet away from the bowl, he has "abandoned" his right to it. Take it away.

From this point onward, moisten all treats with your saliva before giving them to him. Also, put your saliva in his food bowl before he eats from it. This simulates the regurgitation of food or mouth feeding by an adult dog for a puppy. Your dog's acceptance acknowledges his lower status in the "pack."

Using food, or water, to show you give good advice is another form of control. So, before his next feeding, fill his food bowl a quarter-full with water and put a *small* amount of canned dog food in the center of the bowl. Microwave this so that it is just a bit too hot when you test it on your wrist. Call him to you and as he approaches, say "E-a-s-y" in long, drawn-out tones. If he dives in, just stand there. The temperature will startle, but not burn, him. Repeat, "E-e-e-e-a-s-y" before he tries again. Soon he will approach more gently and lick around the edges, which cool first. Say "Good easy" in confident, but assuring, tones. You now have used the feeding ritual in three ways to teach him that you give good advice.

Parading

Periodically, walk past your dog carrying one of his toys, or anything else that the dog likes, close to your face. Ignore the dog. You are doing a shortcut version of pack leader behavior called "parading" that says you are in control. If the *dog* tries parading, either ignore him or take the item away from him. Do not let him make you chase him, however.

Attention Seeking

From now on, never pet your dog if he nudges you for attention. Pet him only on top of his head, back, or muzzle (similar to a handshake). This makes you the top dog in one more way. Petting him *under* the chin or belly makes you the "under dog."

If the dog is either overly timid, or, at the other extreme, an overly dominant take-charge dog, start by petting beneath his chin. Then, throughout several contacts with him, gradually ease your hands to where you are petting him in the top-dog position.

With a dominant dog, stroke his ears back and then stroke his jaw muscles back, so his mouth assumes a "smile." This is a submissive posture in dogs and you reinforce it by petting him at the same time.

Periodically, lay your hand, leg, foot, or arm over your dog's back while he is lying down, sitting, or standing calmly. This is another way to establish your top-dog status. Never let him put his head or paws on you—not even on your lap or your feet. Also, never let a take-charge dog lean on you. Leaning is another form of dominance.

Once you have progressed this far, from time to time stand over your dog, wrap your arms around his belly and lift his front end up toward you. This is a form of a behavior known as mounting and clasping that will also reinforce his submissiveness toward you. When he responds without a struggle, praise him calmly by telling him he's a good dog.

Marking

You may have a male dog whose habit is to "spritz" every tree, pole, and bush in sight when you walk him. Perhaps you have a female who marks territory. Some females even lift their leg much like a male. However, it is more common for a dominant female to lift her leg off the ground under her body. Since this is not as readily noticed, most owners miss this signal of dominant behavior in their female dogs. Whether your dog is male or female, put an end to this behavior. There is little need for a dog to mark territory to make it "safe" when you are in charge.

Walk the dog on leash under your control and allow him (or her) to urinate at the start of every session, but only *once*. If the dog tries marking more than once after he has urinated a good stream, firmly say "No mark!" and head sharply in a direction that will unbalance the dog. Say nothing after that. Just proceed with your walk. Soon the dog will get the idea that you are truly in charge and will need only an occasional "No mark!" delivered sharply when the situation arises.

Eye Contact

Periodically, when no training is going on, stare directly at the dog. Do not look away. It's a human-to-dog variation of the old game that says the one who looks away first loses. In this case, the one who stares the longest is "top-dog."

However, when obedience training you will need to teach your dog to watch your face for signals. He should only do this at your command to "Watch me."

Summary

These interactions are not difficult. In fact, you probably already do some of them with your dog. The key is to do them all and to be consistent. With a timid dog, you may want to do the opposites of the transactions described for establishing leadership over dominant dogs. In the early stages of working with a timid dog, this will help build the dog's confidence. Then over time you can gradually begin interacting the same way that you would with a bolder dog.

Teach your dog to remain calm around toddlers. Photo © Robert and Eunice Pearcy.

Teaching the Basics

As you have seen, your everyday relationship with your dog will determine how well he
listens and obeys. For Bowser to succeed with
Baby, you must have control over him. You must
understand a dog's communications signals and know that
your dog has a pecking order and regards himself as part of
your pack. Teaching a dog to respond to obedience commands
will not solve all your dog's behavior problems, but teaching
sit, down, stand, come, and heel are essential to success.

If you have tried making a dog obey in the past and it has
not worked, there may be several reasons. Here are a few:
Harsh corrections can cause some dogs to fear their owners and
some even learn to punish back. Further, if a dog is constantly
anxious about impending pain or harsh corrections, he may
have a difficult time learning anything new.

From now on, ease into your dog's training in a way that
builds cooperation before he even realizes what is happening—
regardless of his previous behavior or responses to training.
Catch him in the act of doing something you want him to learn,
give this action a command, then praise him for it.

Practice this technique for the next week to ten days—even
as you follow the advice on Rapport Skills™—and you should
see a clear difference in your dog's responses. This could help
save your dog from a dead-end trip to the local humane shelter.

Behavioral Teaching Techniques

There are three ways you can teach your dog to behave in a socially acceptable manner.

The first technique you will be using is called overlaying. You simply watch the dog whenever possible, catch him in the act of doing something right, make him think it was your idea, then reward him for it.

Overlaying

Just as the dog is about to sit, for example, say the word, "Sit," in soothing tones, gently enough that the dog is not distracted from sitting. As he completes the action, say "Good sit." Do the same as he begins to lie down and say, "Good down." Don't use Bowser's name. It might distract him from completing the action. Also, from now on, never say "Down" when you mean to say "Off." It confuses the dog.

After doing the overlaying for a few days, try stroking the top of your dog's head lightly as additional praise. If he gets up, let him. Do not punish incorrect performance at this stage; you are trying to help Bowser make a pleasant association between your words and his specific actions.

Soon, you should be able to get the dog's attention, say either "Sit" or "Down" in the same friendly voice tones, and the dog will assume the proper position, knowing that your praise, "Good sit" or "Good down," comes next. Never force your dog to sit or lie down as part of a punishment. These commands are too valuable to waste in that way.

You can also use overlaying to teach the come. When your dog is coming toward you, whether at random for his dinner or for any other reason he regards as pleasant, say "Come" in an inviting way. Do this as the dog is already in motion, just as you gave the stationary sit and down commands as he was in the act of sitting or lying down. Be sure to sound friendly. When he gets to you, say "Good come," and pat his side. If he turns aside before coming all the way to you, let him. Once again, you are teaching, not correcting.

Through gradual association over a week or so, the dog will begin to respond when you give the commands, even when he was not planning to sit, lie down, or come to you. Conditioning will have taught him that a certain word-sound leads to a certain action on his part and ends with praise from you.

Eliciting

As further training, or if your dog has not responded sufficiently to overlaying, try this: Elicit a sit by showing the dog something interesting in your hand, and then step toward him as you raise your hand in a gentle motion toward and above his head. This action will frequently cause the dog to sit back on his haunches so he can see whatever is in your hand. As he starts to sit, say "Sit" in a friendly tone. When he sits, follow with praise. Be sure to say "Good sit," even if he does not sit all the way. In the beginning, reward anything that comes close to the desired behavior. Bowser will be encouraged to try harder and gradually will do a better sit. Forcing him to sit before he has learned to do it through praise builds unnecessary resistance.

If your dog jumps up, however, merely take the object away. Try again after ten seconds, and this time do not raise the object quite so high. If he persists in jumping, try this: Before you elicit the sit, say "Sit, "then go through the body language. Because you have already conditioned the word through overlaying, it will help him to know what you want when you use the eliciting technique. Some dogs learn differently from others and this will help adjust for those differences.

You can also elicit a down after you are certain you have a good rapport with the dog. When he is on a sit, kneel beside him and—with the object in your hand—dive to the floor so that your forearms are flat on the floor as you continue to kneel. This is a play-elicitation gesture among dogs, and the appropriate response for another dog would be to mimic the gesture. Many dogs will also copy your movements.

Over several sessions, each time the dog assumes the down position, gently slip the arm nearest the dog farther and farther over his back as you say "Good down." Then release him at once with "All right."

To elicit a come, get the dog's attention, then quickly back a few feet away, extending your arms in a beckoning motion. You might also clap your hands lightly. As the dog starts to move toward you, say "Good come." Stop backing up, let him reach

Note:

Dogs with dominant dispositions often require more time with the rapport-building exercises before eliciting can be used to teach down.

you, then praise him and release him with "All right." An immediate release will help him to continue to regard coming to you as pleasant. If Bowser stops coming midway to you, turn away from him, say "All right," and walk on. Watch him out of the corner of your eye. He will most likely follow. When he does, avoid looking back, but say "Good come" in a very pleasant voice.

Light Physical Contact

If you have truly done your best with the first two techniques for at least two weeks and your dog is still not responding well, be sure you are completely successful in doing and maintaining the Rapport Skills™. Next, you can try light physical contact. This does *not* mean force. Gentle guidance will work far better than physical force. Physically guiding the dog into the correct posture starts by setting your expectations low enough that your dog will succeed. Precision should come gradually.

Reminder:

Never discipline your dog for what you have not taught him to do. Show him what you want and encourage him to do it correctly. You will have a far more trusting and compliant dog. However, don't expect perfection on the first try.

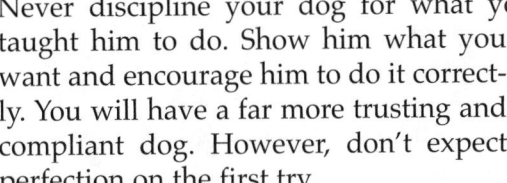 

Teaching Sit and Down Using Physical Contact

Teach the sit first when using this technique. Kneel beside the dog, slip one hand under his collar to restrain him gently, and say the word "Sit" in a pleasant voice. Simultaneously, press your other hand against the back of his hind legs (hocks) and hold his collar lightly with your other hand. This particular point of contact on the dog will cause an "escape" response, meaning that he will move away from the contact rather than push back. As he sits, or even starts to, remove the pressure at once. Say "Good sit," pat him lightly, then release him from the command.

To teach down, first place the dog in a sit. Kneel at his right side, facing in the same direction. Grasp his collar in your left hand and rest your left arm along the dog's back. With your right hand, reach behind his near front leg and grasp the far leg just above the knee. Slide that leg forward, easing the leg nearest you out as well. At the same time, keep gentle pressure on his back and give the command "Down."

Guide your dog into the proper position calmly. If he struggles, do not force him. Time and patience will win him over. If he succeeds, or comes close, praise him, pet him, then release. You can work on duration of the down later.

When using physical contact to teach come, you will need a leash and your dog's regular collar. Hold the lead and stand no more than two or three steps from the dog. With a smile, get his attention. This time, use his name and say "Bowser, Come." Then give the lead a quick tug and release. If you have consistently associated "Come" with pleasure, this should start your dog moving

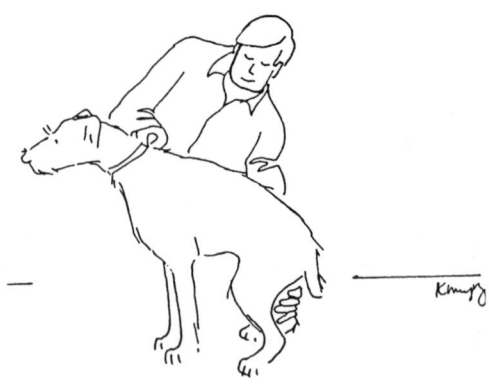

toward you. When he gets to you, praise and pet him briefly and calmly. Then release him.

Caution: Always pause after the verbal command, before you give the quick tug, to avoid stimulating more than one of the dog's senses at a time.

More on Using All Three Methods

This approach will help you teach Bowser that the very presence of the baby is a cue for him to sit.

First teach Bowser how to sit on command in gradual stages. Don't look for polished performance in the first lesson. Make it easy for him to succeed.

Keep the early lessons simple and the following lessons will become even easier. As soon as you finish reading this, start watching Bowser closely. The very second he begins to sit on his own, without any prompting from you, say the word "Sit," in a positive, friendly way. Because he was starting to sit anyhow, he will succeed. You are teaching him that the word "sit" has a certain meaning regarding his motions and posture. Don't use his name at first. It might distract him from sitting. As soon as he

sits, say "Good sit," drawing out the word "g-o-o-o-d." Use soothing tones. Before he gets up, say "All right" to release him from your earlier command.

Bowser is learning that a certain physical act, accompanied by a certain word from you, results in his being praised. He won't give a moment's thought to whether it was your idea or his. He only knows the combination and the end result. After a few days of this, you can begin physically guiding him into the proper position. The association is already there.

At a quiet time, have Bowser stand next to you. Stroke him gently on the back of the head and neck and speak calmingly to him. Pause about five seconds, then say "Sit." Many owners are amazed to find their dog will sit at once, often moving as though in slow motion.

If this does not happen, face your dog and step toward him, raising your hands from waist-high to chest height, extending your palms upward and your fingers outward. The motion should look like an "I don't know" gesture, only closer to the body. This motion will generally cause the dog to sit without physical contact.

If Bowser still does not sit, kneel on the floor and guide him into a sit as you give the command. Touch his rear hocks and support his chest from moving forward. He should sit. If this also fails, you should attend an obedience class to learn how to enforce your commands.

Regardless of how you teach the command, just as Bowser sits, praise him and release him. You both are winners. Now, repeat the pattern for a few days, then start reviewing the training while you have the doll in the room. Lay the doll down and say "Sit" just as the doll is out of your hands but still where Bowser can see it. Do this several times over the next week or so and he will learn that when you put the baby down, he is to sit. Remember to praise calmly.

Praising Bowser's good behavior when you say "Sit" reinforces his desire to sit whenever you lay the baby down. Now you can start phasing out the verbal "Sit" command and get your dog conditioned to sitting just by the action of putting the baby down.

The Shy or Timid Dog

While all dogs should understand the Rapport Skills™ exercises provided earlier, the shy or timid dog may need special help before he can succeed in a home with a new baby. Recent research indicates that many shy children can learn to become confident, and we believe this applies to dogs as well.

First, be sure you are not showing fear in your own behavior, even if the fear is that your dog might bite someone. The dog will perceive your fear message, but, not knowing you are apprehensive about his possible behavior, he may react by becoming even more fearful. In desperation, some dogs may bite out of fear in a misguided effort to protect their "pack," which could be you and your child. Always maintain your top-dog leadership role so that your dog feels confident in your ability to do the protecting.

Next, cease doing anything that has intimidated your dog in the past. This could involve certain ways of playing with your dog, or ways of punishing the dog for behaviors you don't like. It could involve certain people, objects, places, or even situations. Whatever causes the spookiness, prevent it from occurring and keep your dog out of fearful situations.

Study the signals for fear behavior in dogs that we covered earlier in this book. Learn them so that you can head off problems at the first sign. Does he lay his ears back, lower his tail, hunch his shoulders, look away, or begin slinking? Do the whites of his eyes begin to show? Does he wrinkle his brow? Do his eyes begin darting around to look for an escape route?

When working with a shy dog, do not punish him for disobeying commands. Follow the techniques for teaching commands and correcting minor misbehaviors that are contained in this book. They work for all dogs. If your dog becomes spooky, totally ignore him. Never reassure a timid dog with petting or soothing words—it makes the behavior worse because it actually praises the dog for being fearful.

 Never allow a dog that is showing fear of a baby or toddler loose in the same room until the dog has learned to overcome his fearfulness. And never, under any circumstances, leave a fearful dog and a child together unattended.

If your dog is releasing urine out of fear, build his confidence in your leadership through the guidance provided here. If he urinates out of submissiveness, he is carrying out a natural behavior intended to show his regard for your higher status. In either case, arrange to greet him in a location where the urine will not be as much concern to you until you can overcome the problem. You can also crouch or kneel to present a lower, less-intimidating profile.

Put the dog in another room before you clean up the urine or any other mess. While we have no scientific basis for recommending this, we have found that the problem seems to be resolved more quickly when you put the dog out of sight.

In the early stages of working with a timid dog, you should allow—even encourage—the dog to assume dominant postures over you. Initially, encourage him (don't force him) to put his paws or head on you as you both lie on the floor. As he begins to develop confidence, you should begin to phase this out.

When you pet a timid dog, start on his side and under his chin. Stroke his ears into positions that display more confidence. Stroke the tail from the underside, encouraging him to raise it higher. Praise him for each slight improvement. Praise any behavior that even slightly resembles confidence. The word "G-o-o-o-o-d," spoken in long, drawn-out tones, will get the message across. In early training, small treats can be used to accelerate the process.

Plan many good times with your dog, tossing balls or sticks or doing whatever the dog associates with fun. Take him with you to more places if you are certain he will behave. In extreme cases, ask your veterinarian to refer you to a dog behaviorist who can show you how to help your dog overcome specific fears.

Learning to help. Photo © Click the Photo Connection.

Why Punishment Doesn't Work

Why is it always easier to tell people what
not to do, rather than what to do? Perhaps as
some psychologists tell us, by only telling people
what is "wrong" we can avoid responsibility for
almost any alternative they attempt. Some people say it is
because we, ourselves, may not know, or be certain of what is
right.

When a dog does the wrong thing, some owners punish
them. They hit the dog, twist the ear, yank on a pinch collar, or
even shock the dog. Yet, behavioral studies by Dr. Scott and
others show that punishment often does not work at all, or if it
does, the effects are short-lived. If punishment were effective,
the undesirable behavior would permanently change.

However, punishment rarely is effective, and not for long if
it is. It comes after the fact. You can't punish a dog now for what
he did beforehand. Even ten seconds is long enough for a dog
to fail to make the connection. The most timely punishment
only reprimands the dog for what the dog did wrong. It does-
n't give him the slightest clue about what he needs to do to succeed in the future. Suppose your dog could understand. He still
cannot change his past action or project the meaning of punishment into the future.

Dogs do not reason or plan ahead. If a dog chases a squirrel,
punishment does not tell him he must change his behavior the
next time he sees a squirrel. Dogs live only in the present, the
here and now. They have no concept of what humans think of
as "next time."

At best, punishment and yelling may teach a dog to stop in
the act of chasing a squirrel if you yell the same command you

used as you punished him in the past. But what does that teach? Only that yelling is followed by punishment and that he might avoid the punishment he received last time if he stops when you yell. This is a form of what I call "associative learning." One thing becomes associated with the other.

If you are "lucky," that is the response you will get. The dog will stop chasing the squirrel he has already harassed, but only when you yell at him. In reality, the punishment and the yelling have taught him nothing about leaving squirrels alone. In fact, punishing him in the presence of a squirrel could even cause him to fail more in the future because he will be so absorbed in anticipating punishment that he may fail to concentrate on heeling. This leads to more corrections, more stress, and more failure. Think about things you have tried to accomplish under stress and failed, but then succeeded at later when the stress was gone.

Another problem with punishment is that you may be inadvertently punishing the wrong thing. For example, if you punish a dog for racing out the door barking at a stranger, what are you actually punishing? Barking? Or chasing? Even if you still decide to resort to punishment, you can properly train only one thing at a time. In this case, if the dog understands the punishment, he is likely to stop sounding warning barks—an attribute you might want him to maintain.

Suppose you set the dog up to do a five-minute sit at his food dish and he dives in after one minute? Will he understand that you are punishing him for breaking the command? Not necessarily. He may think you are punishing him for eating.

The Rolled-Up Newspaper Syndrome

Even well-meaning people sometimes resort to hitting their dogs with rolled-up newspapers, stuffing their dog's nose into messes on the floor, and so on. Perhaps they are reacting out of frustration and are not truly punishment-oriented. Nevertheless, punishment is punishment.

Yet, canines (wolves, foxes, coyotes) don't resort to any of this type of behavior when they want to take charge of other members of their packs. They assume leadership and seldom have to resort to punishment to get their point across. Humans are the only species preoccupied with trying to find the ultimate punishment for dogs.

Tragically, because of the way most punishment occurs, owners are deluded into thinking it works—even if it only works some of the time. I've seen enough clients who used punishment training that I believe punishment—like gambling—is addictive. It works just often enough to reinforce those who continue to use it.

When people become convinced that punishment works, they have fallen victim to what behaviorists call "superstitious learning." They are convinced that what they are administering is causing the desired outcome when, in fact, something else actually brought about the change, often despite the punishment. In most cases, what really happened was that the dog was exposed to the situation enough times that he finally figured out what he was supposed to do, not what he was punished for *not* doing.

People who punish often go on punishing one dog after the next, even if several dogs in the future fail to learn or are ruined in the process. Here's how it might occur in dog training. In order to set the dog up to be punished, the trainer has to put the dog in the same situations over and over again. This may explain why so many trainers stress repetition. To get any results, they have had to repeat the same lesson over and over, while punishing the dog for mistakes he was never taught to avoid. Logically, after enough exposures to a situation, some dogs will figure out what the trainer expects of them and perform correctly. However, the trainer will conclude that it was the repetition and punishment that taught the dog.

I asked one trainer whether he felt his punishment methods were effective. He immediately pointed to the few dogs that succeeded in competition. The others? He had difficulty even thinking about, let alone talking about, what happened to the others. Question any trainer who uses punishment as his or her primary teaching tool and you may see a defensive reaction that can border on hostility toward you. You can be sure this is an individual who believes that harsh training methods work best.

In dog training, we seem to have forgotten that "discipline" and "disciple" share the same Latin root word "discipulus." A disciple is a follower or student. A disciplinarian is technically a person who trains another in self-control, orderliness, character, and efficiency. The meaning "to punish" is far down the list of definitions for "discipline."

In her excellent book, *Don't Shoot the Dog,* Karen Pryor says that when we think of discipline as punishment, we start thinking, "Do as I say, or else..." in an effort to gain control. Unfortunately, because of poor teaching techniques, the dog has to do something wrong to find out what "or else" means. By then it's too late for him to undo what he has already done.

Is Punishment Ever Effective?

When punishment must be used, it should be remote, event-directed, rather than something the dog associates with the trainer. The goal of such punishment should be to cause the dog to stop the behavior because he thinks his own action produced negative consequences.

For example, if a dog is yelled at by his owner for raiding the wastebasket he will most likely avoid wastebaskets only when the owner is nearby to enforce obedience. On the other hand, a dog that thinks that going into the wastebasket causes a pile of empty tin cans to come crashing down on him, soon learns that wastebaskets, themselves, are "dangerous" and stays clear of them.

Granted, some people will insist that physical, direct punishment has a role in dog training. However, it may be "superstitious learning," at work again. The dog has actually learned *despite* the punishment. However, when punishment doesn't work, you can end up with a punishment-elicited aggressive dog that has to be put down.

Most people who punish, however, resort to even more severe punishment when they recognize that the original punishment didn't work. They fail to try another approach because they don't know what else to try. They lack what behaviorists call "requisite variety." They need to learn effective alternatives to punishment methods. Are we so short of imagination that we can't find something that works better?

A Better Way

What is the better way to train? Behavior modification based upon positive reinforcement. In other words, using a gradual, systematic approach to teach the dog how to succeed at each task, one step at a time, correcting (not punishing) him only up to the level he has already learned successfully. For decades, such positive training methods have been proven to work more successfully.

I encourage trainers to use my Starfire System© to accomplish this because it removes all the guesswork and provides a highly successful way to isolate each part of training so that it can be taught systematically. In particular, my system divides each stationary command into four different parts which we call the 4 D's of dog training and it applies to all breeds.

First we train the dog to hold stationary commands for a gradually increasing *duration* starting at ten seconds and building up to several minutes.

Then we cut the duration requirement in half to make it easier for the dog to succeed as we start having him hold the command at varying *distances*. We start right next to the dog and work our way out to about twenty feet from his side.

Next, we cut the distance requirement in half and take the dog through various *degrees of difficulty*. This begins with the direction the trainer moves to or from the dog, working counterclockwise from the dog's right side, and finally going out of sight. In later training, it also includes issuing the command while the dog is heeling, and while he is coming toward you.

We then ease up on the other requirements and begin to teach *distractions*. We start with general distractions that occur some distance from the dog and work up to where the dog can hold the command even as we create the highest level of distractions.

Follow this positive approach, and others like it, to teach your dog how to succeed and you will avoid the punishment trap that takes its toll on dogs and owners. Moving from one small success to another builds confidence and trust in both dogs and their trainers. It is the most humane way to train, and is also faster, more effective, and more lasting.

Good training makes raising your baby a happy experience.

Correcting Minor Problems

A few general rules can help to reduce or eliminate minor behavioral problems such as nudging to be petted, grumbling to be let out, and other nuisance behaviors. Naturally, general advice will not always work for all dogs and all owners. Specific factors contributing to the problem sometimes need to be taken into account.

However, here are three approaches that can be tried in absolute safety, even if the dog has a dominant personality. That would include the dog whose owners say such things as, "He'd never let me get away with that," "Buzzbomb will only eat sautéed calf's liver," "He wouldn't like it if I tried to sit in that chair. It's his chair," and the list goes on.

The Problem with Scolding

If the dog is trying to write his own rule book in the home, there are several difficulties with attempting to scold as a means of stopping a behavior you dislike. First, if the dog has become truly dominant, he is likely to scold back. He may growl, snap, or even bite. If your dog demands to be fed, then growls if you stand too near the dish you filled for him, scolding could prompt your dog to make a rather severe response.

Some owners attempt to punish their dogs with a light tap on the nose. This could actually confuse the dog because a tap is one of the ways dogs elicit play, yet your voice tones may suggest anger. Even if the dog is not confused, the tap probably will not convince the dog to cease the behavior.

To get more certain, positive results, you must work within the dog's natural instincts. Make him believe you are top dog in his pack, then take humane and appropriate measures to bring about a change in his behavior.

Here are three approaches that work.

The Extinguishing Method

With a minor behavioral problem, the best approach is to keep the dog out of the situation where the behavior has occurred for a period of time and see whether it will go away. Technically called *extinguishing*, this method of not allowing the opportunity for a minor negative behavior to occur, or not giving in to it when it does occur, can often cause the dog to stop doing whatever you wish to terminate. If he can't carry out the behavior, or if his behavior simply doesn't produce the results he intended, he will usually try something else. Just be sure you channel his alternatives into a behavior you will find acceptable.

The Orienting-Reflex Method

Once you have tried extinguishing, a process that could take weeks, you will either be successful or you will be ready to replace the technique or add something else to it. Here is another approach that is safe for both dog and owner. To cause an "orienting reflex" is simply the behaviorists' way of saying "distract your dog." However, the dog should not know that you caused the distraction.

If you are already trying to deal with a minor misbehavior you don't like, you should have a fairly good idea of when and why Bowser behaves as he does. For example, if he frequently comes over to you and complains to go for a walk just as you sit down to your first cup of morning coffee (and you have given in on past occasions), you know what is coming next. This time you will be ready to do something about the chain of events that you have helped condition in your dog. Set up the surprise ahead of time. Collect about a dozen empty food cans and punch two holes in the side of one of them, directly across from each other. Take about fifty feet of strong, nylon cord and tie one end through the holes in that can.

It is important that you carry out the next part where your dog cannot see you. As far away from your coffee as possible, but still in the same room, place the tied can down on something high and flat, like a countertop. Stack another can on top of it, then place a cookie sheet on top of that. Now, as precariously (correct!) as possible, place all of the other cans on the cookie sheet.

Run the nylon cord behind or around something sturdy that will not snag and then bring it directly to your place at the table. (You can run the cord directly to the setup, but it will be easier for your dog to figure out that you are responsible when the trap is sprung.) When your dog gets his nuisance act going, give the cord a discreet tug so the dog does not see you do it. At the same time, ignore the dog and say nothing. Especially avoid the temptation to say, "Boy are you in for a surprise, turkey!"

Suddenly, in the midst of his moaning, the cans come crashing down to the floor several feet away from him. Either ignore whatever happens or jump up, say "What was that!" in a controlled voice, and go investigate. Expect your dog to run, hide or investigate with you. If he races over and attacks the cans, or if he cowers and urinates on the floor, your dog has a problem that warrants the counsel of a professional animal behaviorist.

Make certain the dog is out of the room before you reset the trap again. He should not see you set up or clean up. After the first few exposures, change locations so the dog continues to be caught off guard.

With your trap ready again, allow the dog back into the room and sit down to your coffee. As you start drinking it, your dog will most likely start pestering again. Quietly tug the string. Repeat the entire investigation routine and put the dog out of the room before resetting the trap.

Do this two or three times in a session for the next several days and your dog will learn that the predictable patterns from the past have changed. Now the sequence ends with a loud noise and an investigation rather than with Bowser getting his own way. Periodically, have the setup ready, just in case, so that the dog will never know when starting up his nuisance act will trigger the orienting noise.

You can also rig this device up so the dog trips it himself when trying to steal food off counters, raid garbage cans, enter forbidden areas, and so on.

The orienting-reflex method can be used to break up an undesired behavior in another way. Purchase two or three of the small, hand-held air horns that are available in hardware and marine-supply stores. Keep one in each room where the dog's undesired behavior is likely to occur. Never let the dog see you pick up, or use, the horns.

When the dog is about to get into trouble, hold the horn behind you and blast it sharply. Don't look at the dog. Don't say anything to him. Simply ignore anything he does for the next ten to fifteen seconds. Thus distracted, he is unlikely to return to what he was doing. Now you can call him to you in a friendly tone of voice and pet him for coming.

When a behavior pattern is broken up often enough with such distractions, it becomes less likely that the dog will continue the behavior. But don't overuse the air horn or it will lose its effectiveness.

The Counter-Conditioning Method

This is yet another technique you can use to correct minor problems with a take-charge or spoiled dog. You will have to exercise a little more thought and caution to take into account your dog's personality. The concept basically says that whenever you stop a dog from doing something, you should teach him to do something else.

You must have enough control over your dog that he will listen and obey whatever you choose to teach him. Also, be certain you can teach him an alternative behavior successfully.

A classic example of counter-conditioning is to teach a dog to stop jumping up on people by requiring him to sit instead. Counter-conditioning, when done appropriately, can be successful within a matter of days—especially when accomplished by an overall behavior-modification program.

Let's go back to the "grumbler" again. You are just about to take your first sip of coffee when Take-Charge Bowser decides it is time for you to go for a walk with him. This time you do not ignore his protests and you do not create any distracting noises. You simply give him a command that you know he understands, and then enforce it—the first time. Earlier in this book we have covered three humane ways to teach sit and other commands.

If your dog knows sit, for example, tell him to sit—one time only. Do not repeat the command. Give him precisely ten seconds to obey. That is being more than reasonable with a dog that already knows the command. If he sits, give him modest praise and then immediately release him from the command.

If your dog disobeys more often than he obeys, put him in a collar and make the proper correction to enforce the sit. If you are not certain how to make the correction, or feel the dog might be aggressive toward you, consult an animal behaviorist in your area.

Whether your dog performed correctly and earned praise, or disobeyed and required a correction, immediately go back to your coffee and say nothing more to him.

If you repeat this process often enough, your dog will learn that his grumbling leads only to a sit command, and a correction if he doesn't obey. Thus, you are correcting the dog for a clear-cut failure to follow your instructions rather than for the grumbling. Breaking a pattern in which the dog has decided to take charge usually is a relatively simple task as long as you are patient and persistent. Occasionally the problem will be more serious and require an in-depth program of behavior modification.

Photo © Robert and Eunice Pearcy.

About the Author

Stephen C. Rafe is the founder of Starfire, an organization that has specialized in the study and teaching of behavior-based communications in animals and humans since 1982. He has extensive practical background in the psychology of verbal and non-verbal communication, having studied this subject at both the undergraduate and graduate levels. Since 1982, he has received referrals from some 200 veterinarians to assist owners whose dogs have had behavior problems.

Steve is a former member of Animal Behavior Society and the Dog Writers Association of America. He received a Bachelor of Science degree from Monmouth University, and a Master of Science degree from Marymount University and is currently a doctoral candidate at the University of Phoenix. A specialist in learning theory and nonverbal communication, Steve has also studied the behavioral science of neurolinguistics at the master-practitioner level and has pursued independent research and study in behavior and psychology at the post-graduate-level.

He has published more than 300 by-lined articles in major national and international publications for dog owners, professional trainers, and canine behaviorists. These include: *The AKC Gazette, AKC Afield, Animal Behavior Consultant Newsletter, Capers — Canine Behavior Newsletter, Dog World, Dog Fancy, Dogs of Canada, Off-Lead, Kennel*

Steve and Starfire's Luke Skywalker.

Doctor, several outdoors and sporting publications, and numerous national breed publications. He has been a contributing editor (dog behavior and training) for *Quail Unlimited* magazine since 1987 and was a regular contributing writer to *Off-Lead* magazine for several years.

His book *Training Your Dog for Birdwork* (Denlinger's Publishers, 1988), was nominated as 1988 Training Book of the Year by the Dog Writers Association of America and is now in its fourth printing. He is also the author of numerous pamphlets and manuals on canine behavior and training. He has spoken at the American Boarding Kennels Association national conference, the Outdoor Writers Association of America (OWAA), and the Association of Pet Dog Trainers national conference. He has designed and conducted seminars on canine behavior and training throughout the United States, in Canada, and in South America—including a week-long program for the largest dog-training club in Venezuela. He has also designed and conducted canine-behavior seminars for shelter personnel and volunteers, and for dog owners with children. The latter were sponsored by St. Hubert's Giralda and a regional office of the Humane Society of the United States.

Contact Information:

Stephen C. Rafe
STARFIRE
P.O. Box 8241
Reston, VA 20195

Email: rapport@comcast.net
Website: http://www.starfire-rapport.com

ML   S/05